Stewie Scraps

Top Secret

Photocopiable Worksheets for Enhancing the

Stewie Scraps Stories

Sheila M Blackburn

Brilliant
PUBLICATIONS

Publisher's Information

Brilliant Publications
www.brilliantpublications.co.uk

Editorial Office
Unit 10, Sparrow Hall Farm,
Edlesborough,
Dunstable, Bedfordshire, LU6 2ES, UK
Tel: 01525 222292
Fax: 01525 222720
e-mail: info@brilliantpublications.co.uk

The name 'Brilliant Publications' and the logo are registered trade marks.

Written by Sheila M Blackburn.
Cover illustration and inside illustrations by Leighton Noyes.

© Sheila M Blackburn and Brilliant Publications 2010

Printed ISBN 978-1-905780-75-4
e-book ISBN 978-0-85747-005-8

ISBNs for Stewie Scraps and the ...

Space Racer	978-1-903853-84-9	e-book 978-0-85747-192-5
Easy Rider	978-1-903853-85-6	e-book 978-0-85747-193-2
Giant Joggers	978-1-903853-86-3	e-book 978-0-85747-194-9
Star Rocket	978-1-903853-87-0	e-book 978-0-85747-195-6
Trolley Cart	978-1-903853-88-7	e-book 978-0-85747-196-3
Super Sleigh	978-1-903853-89-4	e-book 978-0-85747-197-0
Set of 6 books	978-1-903853-90-0	
6 sets of 6 books	978-1-903853-91-7	

First printed in the UK in 2010
10 9 8 7 6 5 4 3 2 1

If you would like further information on any of our other titles or to request a catalogue, please visit our website **www.brilliantpublications.co.uk** or telephone **01525 222292**.

Contents

Introduction

Top Secret is a teacher's resource to accompany the Stewie Scraps series of reading books. This book contains photocopiable worksheets for pupils to complete after they have read each of the books in the set. Stewie Scraps has been written in such a way that there is no particular order in which they should be read; each has its own individual storyline.

The sheets can be used after reading each book while the story is still fresh in their minds, or after all the stories have been completed. Included at the front of each section are teacher's notes, which introduce and give advice about each photocopiable sheet. They give suggestions about how to use the stories to develop reading skills and how to make the best use of the worksheets, promoting both written and artistic skills!

These photocopiable worksheets are written and designed to be pupil-friendly, creating an enthusiastic and willing approach to completing the tasks.

There are 6 activities for each story and a set of comprehension questions to help evaluate and assess how well each pupil has understood the story.

The Stewie Scraps stories are supported by a website: **www.stewie-scraps.co.uk**. On the site, children can read the first chapters of each book; find out about Stewie and his family, the author and the illustrator; look at 'Top Secret' stuff; contact Stewie and even enter competitions.

Meet the characters

Stewie Scraps:

Age: 10

Likes: Design and technology – making things out of the junk in his Dad's second-hand shop.

Dislikes: School, especially English, maths and sport.

Family: Mum – Flo, Dad – JJ, sister – Poppy, brother – Clint and Grandpa.

Pets: Bugzy – a brown rat.

This is me: Stewie Scraps, looking at Clint's bike magazine.

This is my Mum, Flo.

This is my Dad, JJ.

This is my sister, Poppy.

This is my brother, Clint.

This is my Grandpa and this … is my pet rat Bugzy.

 ©Sheila Blackburn and Brilliant Publications

Stewie Scraps Top Secret – Teacher's resource sheets for Stewie Scraps

Meet the Characters (continued)

This is my teacher,
Mr Melling.

This is Miles Kingston-Brown.

This is Alfie Battersby.

This is Alfie's Mum.

This is the man from the
Zoomwell Kart Track waving his flag!

This is Connie — she knows
all about trolley karts.

This is Bric-a-brac, she's our dog.

This is Cast-off, he's our cat.

Stewie Scraps Top Secret – **Teacher's resource sheets for Stewie Scraps**

Stewie Scraps and the Space Racer

Stewie spends all week wishing that Friday afternoon would come. It is "Art and Craft" on Friday afternoons, the only lesson Stewie willingly takes part in. When Mr Melling announces the start of a new project on space, Stewie knows exactly what to design, a spacecraft.

After school, Stewie rushes home with his prototype. He can't wait to build the real thing. "We just need a few extra bits on the landing gear ... and then ... all systems go – tomorrow night," he tells Bugzy, his pet rat.

©Sheila Blackburn and Brilliant Publications

Teacher's notes

Task Sheet 1 Forming an argument/giving an opinion
- Read chapter 1: Grand plans.
- List/discuss key points about Stewie at school.
- Do the same for Stewie at home.
- Through discussion and focus questions, encourage pupils to explain why Stewie feels as he does.
- Model how Stewie's views can be turned into sentences.
- Discuss use of first/third person and decide which would be more effective to complete the sheet.

Task Sheets 2 and 3 Looking at characters
- Read chapters 2 and 3: Mission control and Busy day.
- Identify and focus on parts where Stewie is with his family.
- Discuss how they talk to each other/what they say.
- In each space on the sheet, list adjectives or descriptive phrases for each character.
- Choose a character, and complete a sentence that might be spoken by Stewie expressing his feelings and explain with a clause starting with *because*, for example: My sister Poppy is totally crazy *because* she goes out with the weirdest looking boys.

Task Sheet 4 Writing a setting
- Teacher to ask and explain what sentences and paragraphs are.
- Skim through chapters 2 and 3, and focus on parts where the shed is described.
- Collect descriptive words and phrases and write them down in the roof space of the shed on the pupil sheet.
- Read through the collection together.
- Discuss what a paragraph is.
- Model how to use the collected phrases to write a paragraph about the shed as a setting – perhaps give support with ideas for opening sentence.

Task Sheet 5 Definitions
- Discuss special vocabulary and terms/jargon and why it's used.
- Consider other examples, such as mobile phone vocabulary etc.
- Look in a dictionary to see how definitions are given.
- Explain why there is sometimes more than one definition.
- Model one or two parts of the task and encourage pupils to refer to pages and think about the context to devise the definition.

Task Sheet 6 Descriptive comparisons – Similes and metaphors
- Skim and scan the listed pages to find and discuss the examples.
- Discuss how making the comparisons can help and improve the description.
- List some examples such as: as cool as a cucumber, etc.
- Practise orally ideas for some of the listed items, so that pupils know how to reference from the text.

Comprehension
- 12 questions to assess and evaluate how well each pupil has understood the story.

 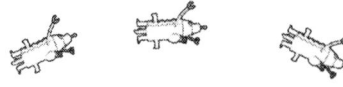

Forming an argument/giving an opinion

Read through chapter 1, *Grand Plans*. Write down in the top frame what Stewie thinks about his school. Now write in the bottom frame what Stewie thinks about his home and family.

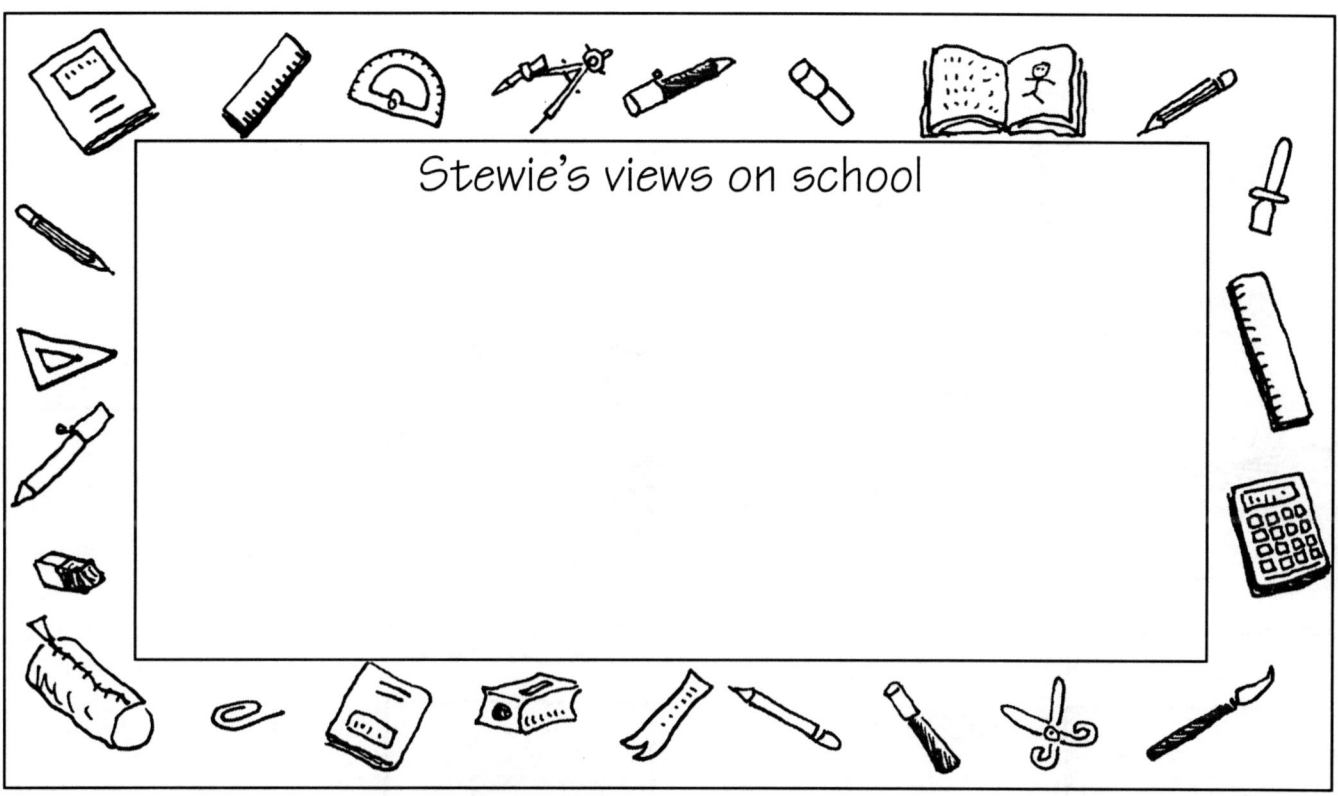

Stewie's views on school

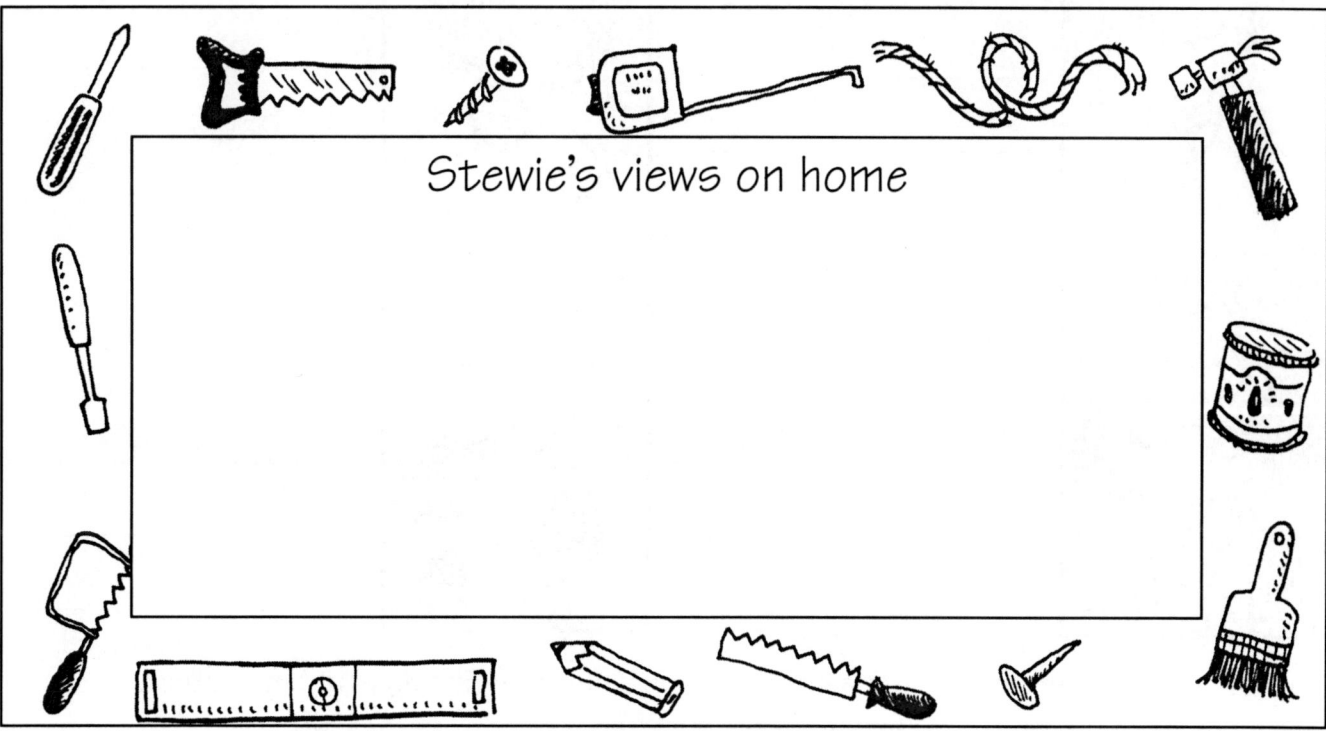

Stewie's views on home

©Sheila Blackburn and Brilliant Publications

 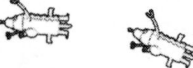 

Looking at characters

Read through chapters 2 and 3, Mission control and Busy day. Beside each of the boxes below, write down a list of adjectives or descriptive phrases for each of these characters.

Stewie

_____

_____

_____

J.J.

_____

_____

_____

_____

Grandpa

_____

_____

_____

Poppy

_____

_____

_____

_____

Flo

_____

_____

_____

_____

Clint

_____

_____

_____

_____

Choose a character and write a sentence expressing how Stewie might feel about them, using the word 'because' ... , ie 'My sister is totally crazy because she ...'.

Looking at characters

Write down a list of adjectives or descriptive phrases for each of these characters.

Mr Melling

_____

_____

_____

_____

Bugzy

_____

_____

_____

_____

_____

Bric-a-brac

_____

_____

_____

_____

_____

_____

Cast-off

_____

_____

_____

_____

 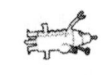
Writing a setting

Read through chapters 2 and 3 again, writing down any descriptive words and phrases you find. Use the outlined area of the shed to store your words and phrases. Now write a paragraph using these descriptive words and phrases to help you.

  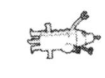

Definitions

Look at the word/phrase listed below, find it in the text and give a brief description of its meaning.

Stewie's technical vocabulary	Definition
Page 11 inter-galactic, robotic braking device	
Page 11 landing pod	
Page 13 prototype	
Page 23 landing gear	
Page 39 cybo-bolt	
Page 39 command console	
Page 43 command seat	
Page 45 hatch cover	
Page 45 over-warp drive	
Page 45 meteor- proof screen	
Page 49 atmosphere read-out	

©Sheila Blackburn and Brilliant Publications

Stewie Scraps Top Secret – Teacher's resource sheets for Stewie Scraps

Descriptive comparisons – Similes and metaphors

Listed in the space racer are some exmples of similes and metaphors. What do you think is meant by them?

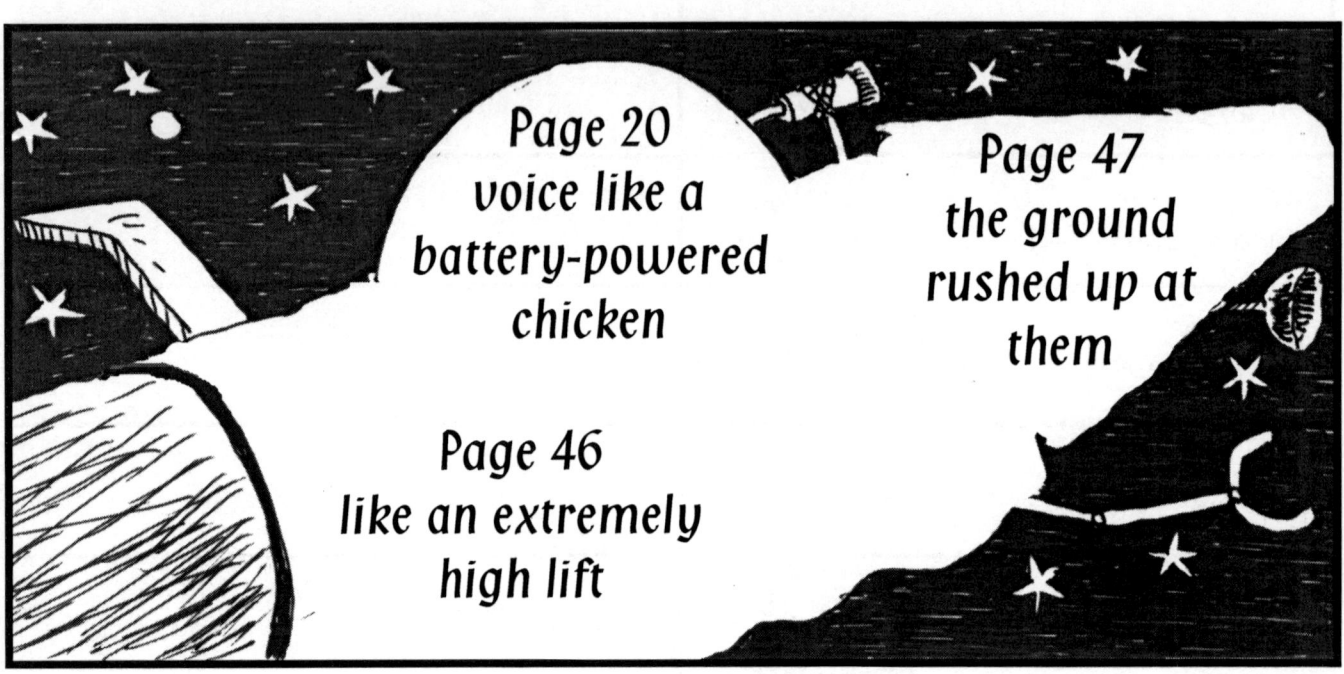

Page 20
voice like a battery-powered chicken

Page 47
the ground rushed up at them

Page 46
like an extremely high lift

Add a metphor or simile to complete the following.

The playground was as _____

Stewie's lessons were _____

Bric-a-brac's coat was _____ like _____

Cast-off was like _____

The shed at the bottom of the yard was _____

JJ's shop was_____

Bugzy trembled like_____

The Space Racer landed like _____

The new planet was_____

The nose cone was burned like _____

 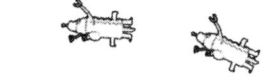
Comprehension

1. Why (on page 5) do you think Grandpa called baby Stewie a little scrap?

2. Suggest why Stewie leaves answering questions to others in class (page 8).

3. Explain why (on page 12) Mr Melling is impressed with Stewie.

4. Poppy often seems to look after Stewie as much as his Mum (pages 20 and 36). Say how she does this.

5. Stewie often goes with JJ and Clint to collect things for the shop. Why is he so useful to JJ (page 27)?

6. What evidence (page 30) is there that Flo works hard in the shop all week?

Comprehension (continued)

7. JJ's shop is open every day of the week. Explain why it's important for business to be open every day and especially Sunday (page 38).

8. Look at the evidence on pages 19, 22, 23 and 36. Can you think of reasons why Bugzy is Stewie's best friend?

9. Compare Stewie's home above the shop in his home town with the new planet. Find words and phrases to show why he thinks it's so beautiful.

10. Why are the eyes angry with Stewie?

11. What lesson does Stewie have to learn on the new planet (page 57)?

12. In your own words, say what you think might have happened at the end of the story.

Stewie Scraps and the Easy Rider

Top Secret.

Easy Rider

Stewie's big brother Clint is always out with his friends on motorbikes.

"Oh, Wow! Come and look at this, Stewie!" calls Clint. It is a beautiful glistening red and chrome motorbike with long steering rods and long cow-horn handlebars!

Later that night, Stewie secretly flicks through Clint's bike magazines until he finds a picture of that bike. Then he does something really daring – he rips the page out of Clint's magazine.

Find out how Stewie builds his own bike and what happens on the Easy Rider's first outing.

©Sheila Blackburn and Brilliant Publications

Teacher's notes

Task Sheet 1 Developing a character – Clint
- Read chapter pages given/skim for parts where Clint is involved.
- With each sighting, make notes/key words that show what Clint is doing and what sort of person this shows him to be. This should be a joint/group/paired task, depending on the children.
- Discuss what has been collected.
- Use dramatic conventions such as hot-seating to find out more of Stewie's actual feelings towards Clint – encourage/model focus questions.
- Model the task and provide support words for writing.
- Share the writing and ask the children to comment on each other's ideas and (if appropriate) to ask questions of each other.

Task Sheet 2 Preparing questions for an interview
- Check that pupils understand questions and answers by playing a game in round: one asks a question and nominates another to give an answer. The one who answers then becomes the questioner. Questions can be about any chosen subject.
- Vary the game by basing the questions on characters in the text/scenes from the text (eg: Grandpa and Stewie in the shed).
- Look at how these would be written down and discuss punctuation.
- Look again at chapter 4 to identify main characters and the events in which each is involved.
- Model task by giving examples of the questions that might be posed to each character selected – stress that because they are to be interviewed by the reporter, the questions are put to them and not asked by each of them.
- After the task, pupils should share their ideas for questioning and use the questions in a short role play – it would be interesting to see if the answers are in keeping with both characters and text (as an indication of comprehension).

Task Sheet 3 Newspaper report
- Look at a selection of newspapers and pick out main features: name, use of fonts, headline, subheadings, text in columns, use of pictures and captions etc.
- Discuss how we report things by looking back and saying what happened – use of past tense.
- Consider punctuation and impact words/short sentences for impact.
- Read through chapter 4 and help pupils to make notes at the top of the page.
- Discuss these and any possible improvements.
- Model the task, perhaps as far as the opening paragraph.
- As pupils prepare their own work, give support with words etc.
- Explain what is meant by a draft – consider this first try as a draft that is to be read and shared with others for peer assessment and chances to improve.
- Add notes to first draft/re-write as a second draft.
- Write final draft. Use a computer to publish as a newspaper front page if possible.

Task Sheets 4 Short playscript
- Look at a playscript together and try to find examples of the following:
  Scene: (chapter title)
  Setting: (description of where play takes place)
  Narrator: (a storyteller who tells us what's gone on before and may introduce the characters)
  Stage notes: in (parentheses)
  How speaker is presented/use of margin.

Teacher's notes (continued)

Task Sheet 4 Short playscript (continued)

- Read chapters 1 and 4 together and choose the one that the class feel gives scope for the best playscript (lots of dialogue and action).
- Go through the text carefully, picking out dialogue/scope for dialogue and actions that will become stage directions.
- Model how the scene might start, including speaking parts and stage directions.
- Begin by asking pupils to give the scene, setting and a piece for the narrator to say by way of introduction.
- Check what's been written and that children have included the elements modelled above.
- Discuss what comes next in terms of who says what.
- When pupils have finished, read each other's scripts and comment.
- Try them out as a play!

Task Sheet 5 Writing from someone's point of view

- Talk about the writer's point of view – writing in third person.
- Look at examples of this on various pages and show the children how it can be changed into the first person: eg, the impartial viewpoint of chapter 1 can be re-written from Clint's point of view, with use of first person.
- Discuss how this would be done for the scene with Clint and Stewie at the window together.
- Identify the key parts of the scene from Clint's point of view and make an ordered list of how things happen.
- Model how the list can be changed into the scene from Clint's view, including both narrative and dialogue; vary sentence length.
- Ask pupils to continue from modelled part – it might be necessary to limit the amount required/give a point in the scene where the task should stop.
- Upon completion, share and discuss the pieces of writing, making constructive comments and asking pupils to suggest ways to improve.

Task Sheet 6 Persuasive writing – poster design

- Collect a number of posters/local newspaper adverts for forthcoming events, especially sports events.
- Compare layout and choice of words/use of font and punctuation.
- Display these on a chart and point out things that posters have in common.
- Discuss essential information of time, date, venue, costs.
- Model the task and a possible layout.
- Pupils' first drafts can be published on computers – try a mix of graphics and own illustrations.
- Share results and ask pupils to be "good buddies" to comment on other posters and what they think will work as a good piece of persuasion.

Comprehension

- 30 questions to assess and evaluate how well each pupil has understood the story.

Developing a character – Clint

Stewie shares a room with his older brother, Clint. He doesn't see very much of him, though this story begins with them together and Clint is an important character. Sometimes, Stewie gets on with him, sometimes not.

Draw a picture of Clint in the frame below and focussing mainly on pages: 5–8, 10–12, 21, 28–34, 62–63, 64 and 65; think of ways that Stewie would talk about Clint and describe him.

Let me tell you about my big brother Clint – he's … _____

_____

_____

Preparing questions for an interview

In this action-packed chapter, Stewie takes part in the night race. You are a newspaper/ TV reporter, getting ready to interview the main characters for your report/news item. Pick two people at the track, draw them in the boxes on this page and then write the questions you would like to ask each of them.

Newspaper report

Read Chapter 4, *Let the race begin*. Imagine that a local newspaper reporter was at the track when Stewie raced the Easy Rider. Help the reporter to write a report about the night's events.

Make notes here to list the main events of the night, in order.

Write some powerful "wow" words here.

Now use your notes and words to write the report here:

Headline

Subheading

Picture

Reporting column

Caption

Reporting column

Short playscript

Use the frame on this page to write your own playscript based on either Chapter 1 *It's curtains for the curtains* or Chapter 4 *Let the race begin*.

Set your playscript out as follows:
Scene: (chapter title)
Setting: (a description of where the play takes place)
Use a Narrator (a storyteller to tell what's gone on before and to introduce the characters).
Put the speaker's name in the left-hand column and write their script (what they say) on the right.

Scene: _____

Setting: _____

_____ _____

_____ _____

_____ _____

_____ _____

_____ _____

_____ _____

_____ _____

_____ _____

_____ _____

_____ _____

_____ _____

©Sheila Blackburn and Brilliant Publications

Writing from someone's point of view

Read Chapters 1 and 4. Imagine Clint was telling the story ... how would he write what happened? Write a brief outline from Clint's perspective of the days events.

_____
_____
_____

_____
_____
_____
_____
_____

_____
_____
_____
_____
_____
_____
_____

_____
_____

_____
_____
_____
_____
_____
_____
_____
_____
_____
_____
_____

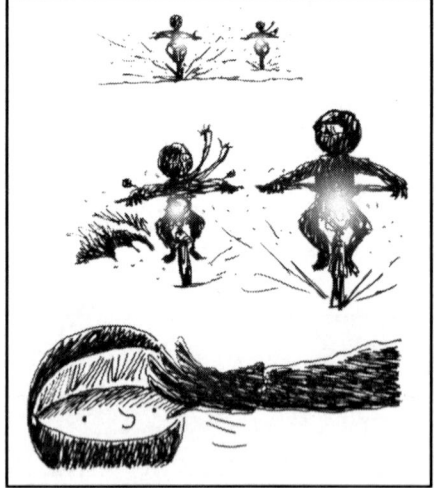

_____
_____
_____
_____
_____

Persuasive writing – Poster design

Look at Chapter 4 *Let the race begin*. In this action-packed chapter, Stewie takes part in the night race. If you were organizing the races at the track, what would your publicity poster look like? What words and information would you use? Think of extra words you would use for impact.

Comprehension

1. Look at page 9. Do you think what Stewie is doing is a good idea? What should he do?

2. Explain what you understand by "if he'd been Cast-off, he'd have rubbed himself against it and purred" from page 10.

3. Reading through page 11. What does Clint do that he shouldn't have done? Why was he wrong – and what could he have done instead?

4. What makes Stewie fall off the pile of books (page 12)?

5. Several things go wrong for Stewie one after the other (pages 14, 15 and 16). Make a list of four or five of those things.

6. Give two or more reasons why Stewie's Mum is cross (page 17).

Comprehension (continued)

7. Look at page 18. What makes Flo forget to be cross with Stewie?

8. Grandpa doesn't seem to be too worried about what happened to Stewie – how do we know this (page 22)?

9. Explain why, on page 23, Grandpa will not accept that Stewie might be missing Clint.

10. Why (on page 23) is Grandpa amazed?

11. (Page 24) Why do you think Grandpa winks at Stewie?

12. Why is Stewie (page 28) suddenly jealous of his brother, Clint?

©Sheila Blackburn and Brilliant Publications

Comprehension (continued)

13.   What has Stewie done, on page 29, to manage things in the shared bedroom?

14.   Why do you think Stewie's head begins to spin (page 33)?

15.   Say why Clint might well be cross with Stewie (page 35).

16.   Why, on page 38, do you think Grandpa isn't surprised to see Stewie out of bed so early?

17.   Why is Stewie happy to avoid his Mum, Dad and Poppy (page 41)?

18.   Why do you think Stewie showed Grandpa the bike picture? What do you think Grandpa meant by "second engineer" (page 43)?

Comprehension (continued)

19. Why was Stewie probably very glad he let Grandpa help? What might Grandpa have done that would have upset Stewie (page 44)?

20. Why, on page 49, do you think Stewie grins a "mean grin"?

21. What does the man mean by "kiddy noises" (page 51)?

22. Say why Stewie (on page 52) only nods and puts his thumbs up at first.

23. How do you think Stewie came up with his racing name? Say what you think about the name (page 54).

24. There are several ways that Stewie seems full of confidence – list them and say how they compare with Stewie back at home and in school.

©Sheila Blackburn and Brilliant Publications

Comprehension (continued)

25. List the ways in which Stewie and the bike champion tease each other (pages 55–56). Why do you think they talk like this?

26. Why does Stewie think his brains are going to burst?

27. What caused Stewie to crash?

28. Clint is angry and not just with Stewie … (page 63). Make a list of all the things he's angry about.

29. Do you think it's just a lucky chance that Grandpa comes to the door at that moment (page 64). Explain your answer.

30. Page 65, sees another of Grandpa's winks at Stewie – what do you think he winks for this time?

Stewie Scraps and the Super Sleigh

Super Sleigh

"Merry Christmas" reads a battered plastic sign in JJ's dusty shop window.

A new boy starts in Stewie's class and they soon become friends. Then Stewie realizes that since Miles came along, he hasn't come up with any new designs.

"That's it," he exclaims. "I've had an idea at last ... . Perfect. Everything I need is here ... . Look at my design"

he tells Bugzy, his pet rat, "The Stewie Scraps Super Sleigh ... bet you can't wait!"

Stewie sits on the driver's seat of the sleigh ... but nothing happens. He tries the next day and the day after that. Still nothing.

What's wrong with the sleigh? Why won't it go anywhere? What else does it need? Where will the Christmas Magic come from?

Teacher's notes

Task Sheet 1 Writing letters

- Read through the first part of the book and discuss the things Stewie might like/need/be able to afford.
- You could scribe the children's ideas in three columns on a chart for discussion.
- It might also be useful to compare a similar list for Miles.
- Help the children to skim and scan for words and phrases for their key words to put in the bell shaped box.
- Look at different letter formats and discuss the appropriate tone and phrasing for this letter – some examples on sticky notes will help pupils to select the right sort of phrases.
- Similarly, look at different ways to end a letter and pick a suitable one for Stewie here.
- If needed, model a letter that Stewie might have written and ask the children how it could be improved/changed and why.
- After the task, ask pupils to exchange their letters and comment on each other's.

(It might be useful to distinguish between a "normal" Santa letter and the typical letter that Stewie would write – as he hates writing so much!)

Task Sheet 2 Ordering words in sentences

- Ask the children to say a sentence about an event such as a birthday, write it down, then chop up the words and muddle the order. This can be done so that it sounds almost right. Discuss what's happened.
- Now give a jumbled word sentence prepared previously and ask the children to sort it into a sensible order – it might be useful to point out that a sensible order is not the same as the right order – there may be alternatives.
- Look at the task sheet together and read the instructions.
- Read and model the first sentence and discuss alternative ordering.
- After the task, read answers together and discuss any differences. – what works and what doesn't?

Task Sheet 3 Adverbs

- Discuss verbs with pupils and then introduce/reinforce adverbs.
- Have a few sticky notes prepared with verbs on and others (in a different colour) with adverbs – ask the children to mix and match these and discuss what effects are achieved if the adverbs are changed.
- Repeat with just one verb and different adverbs, for example walk. Discuss how the adverbs would suggest all sorts of atmosphere and events, like walk happily; walk quickly; walk awkwardly; walk sadly.
- Introduce the sheet and the task and read through together.
- Read all the words in the choice box at the foot of the page.
- Stress that these are not the only adverbs that might be used – also stress how an adverbial phrase such as: with a sigh – can be effective.
- Model the task.
- After completion, ask the pupils to share one or two of their favourite examples

Teacher's notes (continued)

Task Sheet 4 Commas in lists

- Look at basic punctuation such as full stops, capitals, ? and !.
- Introduce/revisit the comma.
- Look at examples of how and where it is used – it might be useful to look in books or have some examples ready on cards or sticky notes.
- Teach the children the rules about commas in lists, ie not before the first word in the list or before the final 'and' at the end of the list.
- Devise some examples together to model – foods at a party make a good example.
- Emphasize the size and position of commas.
- Read through the task and model how to use the page references.
- Look at some of the pages that are to support the sentences.
- Set the task and check together upon completion.

Task Sheet 5 Alphabetical order – First letter

- Look at an alphabet.
- Recite it as a song.
- Play games: find the tenth letter/what comes after or before?
- Put some wooden letters in a bag and pick one out – give the next letter in the alphabet.
- Read through sheet and model task with other lists prepared previously.
- Check work together after the task and exchange pupils' own lists for sorting.

Task Sheet 6 Completing sentences

- Demonstrate how sentences can be completed in an interesting way or in a quick and disappointing way by finishing off this example: In the gloomy shed … .
- Discuss the effects of detail and describing words with pupils and ask them for two or more ways to finish off: Deep in the cold dark night … .
- Read through the task and model the first part, using the page references to support with ideas.
- After completion, share a selection of answers, compare and offer evaluations – encourage pupils to say something supportive and constructive about each other's work.

Comprehension

- 21 questions to assess and evaluate how well each pupil has understood the story.

Writing letters

When reading pages 5–33, you find that one of the important things that Stewie has forgotten to do (or has avoided doing) in the weeks before Christmas is … to write a letter to Father Christmas. Can you think what he might ask for? Jot a few ideas in the bell below.

Next, use your ideas to write a letter to Santa for Stewie.

Ordering words in sentences

Stewie's class – and his school – do a lot of things at the end of term. If Mr Melling had asked Stewie to write about it after Miles left the class, Stewie would probably have had a lot of trouble putting things in order. Can you help him out? Look at the jumbled sentences and put the words into the right order to make the sentence correct.

December beginning of At the the to fit had a big tree into our school our caretaker hall.

_____

_____

Monday hack morning to of It took him all and bits saw off trunk. the

_____

_____

the corridors decorate of snowy branches. and Rows of lights.

_____

_____

time 6 spent Year a lot of to trying reach them.

_____

_____

a silver green Melling Mr my teacher tree brought and into the classroom.

_____

_____

_____

©Sheila Blackburn and Brilliant Publications

Ordering words in sentences (continued)

We decorate it had to but the Melling Mr lights put on.

_____

_____

and metres metres made We chains of paper.

_____

_____

Melling Mr chains hung the the around classroom.

_____

_____

dangled clumps He of tinsel chains from the paper while made
we lanterns paper

_____

_____

classroom Our brilliant looks and Melling Mr has to keep ducking get the room round to.

_____

_____

_____

Adverbs

Read through pages 1–12, 15, 22–25 and 29. There are lots of things going on in December and everyone is busy, including Stewie! Here are some of the events for you to describe by giving or choosing good adverbs to match the activities. Select from the adverbs given at the bottom of the page.

The Christmas lights over JJ's shop counter flickered _____ .

Flo, Poppy and Clint decorated the shop window _____ .

The boxes of stock were piled _____ in the shop and the flat above.

The school caretaker sawed and hacked _____ at the enormous Christmas tree.

Mr Melling ducked and stooped _____ under all the paper chains and lanterns.

The new boy, Miles, did Stewie's work _____ .

When Miles visited JJ's shop, he looked round _____ .

The shed door opened _____ and Bugzy scuttled out _____ .

Miles stroked the old skis _____ .

Back inside the shed, Stewie picked up the old skis _____ .

dangerously   happily   quickly

grumpily   clumsily   awkwardly

roughly   merrily   angrily   carefully

happily   willingly   easily   warily

in dismay   with a creak   lovingly

with a smile   thoughtfully

with a sigh   with a squeak

©Sheila Blackburn and Brilliant Publications

Commas in lists

Stewie's life is full of lists – and not just present lists! Put each of these lists into a sentence. Make sure you remember to use commas.

Example: here is a list of Stewie's pets: Bugzy Cast-off Bric-a-brac
Let's put this information into a sentence:

  Stewie's pets are Bugzy, Cast-off and Bric-a-brac.

Now put each of the following lists into a sentence of your own.

JJ   Flo   Grandpa   Clint   Poppy (chapter 1)

_____

_____

lights   snowy branches   paper chains   tinsel   lanterns (chapter 1)

_____

_____

a length of tinsel   a cotton-wool snowman   a battered plastic sign (pg 6)

_____

_____

maths answers   spellings   story plans   homework (p17)

_____

_____

cross-members sides steering reins seat storage box (pg 37)

_____

_____

Alphabetical order – First letter

Everybody in the story is busy getting things in order. Look at the first letter of each word listed below and put them in order, like the order of letters in the alphabet:

An example of some goodies on the sleigh: **trains books games crayons dolls**
Would be organized as: **<u>b</u>ooks <u>c</u>rayons <u>d</u>olls <u>g</u>ames <u>t</u>rains**.

Now it's your turn with:

lights   branches   chains   tinsel   snowmen

_____

cartons   tins   boxes   sacks   packets   envelopes

_____

nails   hammers   saws   chisels   brushes   pliers

_____

tinsel   lights   bells   crackers   novelties   star   angels

_____

sandy   icy   windy   hot   dry   cold

_____

merry   jolly   happy   cheery   funny   laughing

_____

Make up some lists of your own. Pass it to a friend to arrange in alphabetical order.

Completing sentences

Stewie is surrounded by busy, excited people, wherever he turns. He's also very busy and excited too – sometimes it makes him forget what he was going to say. Help Stewie to finish his sentences by giving a good ending for each one.

Page 21
I feel a bit worried about Miles visiting the shop because

_____

Page 30
Don't worry about old Bugzy – he's

_____

Page 33–35
Miles just isn't my sort of friend – he's too

_____

Page 45
The sleigh's great and I thought it would

_____

Page 52–53
I knew exactly what the ringing sound was – the bell!
It was _____

_____

Page 56
The voice was deep and jolly and I knew

_____

_____

Page 64
No doubt about it … the silver box was

_____

_____

Comprehension

1. Read page 5. Why do you think the lights "worried". Lights don't really have such feelings – this is a metaphor. Is it a good way to describe the lights? Why?

2. Explain why, on page 7, the display in JJ's shop window was only changed twice a year.

3. Looking at page 10, it describes the corridor decorations as "nearly out of reach of Year 6…". Why do you think this might be important?

4. Read pages 11–12. Describe how Stewie's classroom was decorated. Why did it become a problem for Mr Melling?

5. Say why someone sniggered when the new boy was introduced to the class (page 13).

6. Stewie's offer to help the boy might seem odd to some – what do you think?

Comprehension (continued)

7. From pages 16–17, explain why Stewie's new friend is a great advantage to him.

8. Name two differences between Stewie and Miles, as stated on page 18.

9. Explain why Stewie realizes he shouldn't have invited Miles to the shop (page 21).

10. Stewie was cross with Miles – explain why, using two or more reasons from the story (page 26).

11. Read page 29. What do you think makes Miles scared?

12. Stewie can't wait to get rid of his friend (page 33) – do you think this is sad or do you understand how Stewie feels? How do you feel about Miles?

Comprehension (continued)

13. Breaking friends with Miles is a big step for Stewie – can you think why?

14. From pages 40–41, make a list of all the things that Stewie's class friends enjoy at this time of year, but which don't particulary matter to Stewie.

15. Why did Stewie need to hold Bugzy firmly?

16. What do you think Grandpa had in mind when he gave the bell to Stewie?

17. "Christmas Magic" is mentioned both on page 49 by Grandpa and by Stewie on page 53. What do you think they each meant when they used these words?

©Sheila Blackburn and Brilliant Publications

Comprehension (continued)

18. Who do you think Stewie is talking to when he asks this question? (page 55.)

19. Read page 58. This is not happening on Christmas Eve. Can you say why?

20. In a way, Stewie does far better than Miles K-B – and better than Miles ever thought he would. Explain how.

21. What makes you think that this adventure really happened? Or did Grandpa have something to do with it?

Stewie Scraps and the Trolley Cart

A Trolley Cart

Alfie Battersby, just about the cleverest and richest boy in Mr Melling's class, hands Stewie an invitation to his karting-party.

"Wow!"

Stewie is on Alfie's team at the karting track. He tries to remember everything he's been shown but it isn't as easy as he expects – and he isn't the only one having problems!

It is all over far too quickly.

Back at the flat, Stewie heads for the shed as soon as he can. "Got to get it all down before I forget." But his new design doesn't go according to plan. Find out what goes wrong and how Grandpa comes to the rescue.

©Sheila Blackburn and Brilliant Publications

Teacher's notes

Task Sheet 1 Sentence starters

■ Read chapter 1 and discuss Stewie's reactions, worries and different feelings throughout the morning.

■ Role play and some hot-seating might help to establish Stewie's thoughts and reasons.

■ Read through the sheet and discuss the task.

■ Explain to the children that this task is written in the first person, as opposed to the text which is written in the third person – relate this to the role play.

■ Discuss whether one or two words will be enough to complete each sentence.

■ Model one or two sentence endings.

■ After the task, ask pupils to read each other's work and pick out a favourite sentence ending to share.

Task Sheet 2 Nouns and adjectives

■ Revisit adjectives and highlight some on a copy of part of the text.

■ Discuss what the sentences would be like without the adjectives.

■ Prepare some post-it notes with nouns and ask children to give an adjective to go with each. Put the words into sentences orally, then repeat without the adjectives – this might relate to the story or to everyday things that are familiar to the children.

■ Repeat once more with different adjectives and discuss how the sentences have changed.

■ Read through the sheet and discuss the task.

■ Read the adjectives given.

■ Model one or two parts of the task, using the page references to put the words in context and support appropriate choices of adjectives.

■ When the children have finished, compare their choices as a whole group and discuss how different choices can convey different meanings.

Task Sheet 3 Writing an invitation

■ Look at page 7 alongside some pre-printed bought invitations. Discuss what essential elements an invitation must have.

■ Does Alfie's invitation have all these?

■ Think about Stewie in this story – and others – and talk about what we know about him: his likes and dislikes.

■ Give each child a sticky note for writing a good theme party idea for Stewie. This doesn't have to be complicated, as long as the children know they have to talk about aspects of their ideas.

■ Put the notes in the middle of the main table/on a board/in a box and select one at a time – the creator has to be able to talk about the idea in terms of what we know about Stewie and his family. Based on this text, the party could be held in the park with a picnic and trolley cart rides down the slope, turning into a competition … this would be easier for Flo to organize and afford. Other venues might be too expensive, though the choice of themes should not be a problem.

■ Read through the sheet and discuss the task, including appropriate illustrations – these could be based on the ones in the story.

■ Remind the children about writing lists, commas in lists and how to check spellings.

■ After the task, discuss the different ideas and possible outcomes – these might form the basis of further role play and writing tasks.

Teacher's notes (continued)

Task Sheet 4 Connectives
- Visit/revisit connectives by using shorter sentences about everyday school routines.
- Prepare sticky notes with a variety of connectives written on them.
- Demonstrate how the connectives can be used to link sentences.
- Show how the connectives can be placed in different parts of a sentence.
- Read through the sheet together, making sure that children can read and understand the connective words.
- Model the task, trying different connectives in the spaces and discuss which are suitable and why.
- After the task, ask children to look at each other's work, read it and comment on the use of chosen connectives.

Task Sheet 5 Heads and tails
- Demonstrate the way that funny sentences can be made by writing some down, then chopping them in half and mixing up the endings.
- Explain that reading these funny sentences and recognizing they are not right is a sign of good reading – and a useful thing to do when self-checking your own writing.
- Read through the task sheet together and put some of the sentences together incorrectly so that pupils have further chance to say what's wrong.
- Model how to try out different options and then to write the new sentence on the second sheet, paying attention to basic punctuation.
- After the task, read through the new sentences together, discussing any that do not match.

Task Sheet 6 Who said that? – Speech marks
- Copy some parts of texts and highlight the dialogue.
- Look together at the speech marks.
- Draw some speech marks on sticky notes and use them to punctuate dialogue on a whiteboard.
- The above can also be turned into a game with pupils holding parts of a sentence of dialogue and others standing in the correct places with the speech marks.
- Look at use of commas.
- Discuss how dialogue might come first in a sentence, or last after the speaker – look at the use of commas in both cases.
- Make sure that pupils know there are other ways to present and punctuate dialogue – this task only uses the first two formats.
- Read the sheet together and make sure that the children can understand who speaks in each piece of dialogue.
- Model one part of the task, matching the dialogue to the character picture and adding all the punctuation – ask the children if it is correct.
- After the task, invite the children to check a friend's work and comment on their use of punctuation.

Comprehension
- 20 questions to assess and evaluate how well each pupil has understood the story.

Sentence starters

Read through the first chapter. Stewie is so surprised and thrilled to get an invitation from Alfie Battersby, he can hardly speak. Help him to get over his problem by finishing off these sentences for him:

1. I didn't take the envelope off Alfie straight away because

_____

2. Wow! I've got an invitation from

_____

3. I opened the envelope very carefully because

_____

4. Cool! Alfie's invited me to

_____

5. Mr Melling had a hard time this morning – all the boys

_____

6. All morning I thought about all the ways to tell Mum, but

_____

7. I ran back to the shop after school and Mum was

_____

8. Mum looked at the card and looked really serious – I thought

_____

9. Brilliant! Mum's keen for me to go and she says

_____

10. She thinks of everything, my Mum – now she's worrying

_____

Nouns and adjectives

In this story, Stewie has some experiences that take his breath away – and they need describing carefully. Look at the next page and use the imagery for each to write one or two good adjectives (describing words) that will really suit each word.

Unexpected	Untidy	Challenging	Deep
Surprise	Red	Amazing	Busy
Exciting	Curly	Twisty	Detailed
Endless	Interesting	Silvery	Friendly
Noisy	Flashing	Shiny	Calm
Breathless	Bright	Old-fashioned	Wonderful
Desperate	Delicious	Helpful	Scary
Worried	Tasty	Careful	Clear
Secret	Colourful	Labelled	Fun-filled

©Sheila Blackburn and Brilliant Publications

Nouns and adjectives (continued)

The page references will help you to find the words that need describing. Use the adjectives on the previous page to help you fill in the blanks … unless you can think of better ones yourself!

Page

7   The _____ , _____ invitation

9   The _____ , _____morning in school

10   Stewie's _____ , _____ dash home

16   The _____ , _____ design book

30   The _____, _____ karting sign

33   The _____, _____ food tables

34   The _____, _____ track

43   The _____, _____ races

46   The _____, _____ trophy

51   Grandpa's _____, _____ sketches

55   The _____, _____ slope

57/58   A _____, _____ girl

59   A _____, _____ afternoon

Writing an invitation

Look at Alfie's invitation to the Zoomwell Karting Track. Imagine Stewie was having a party. What sort of party would it be and where would he have it? Help him to write the invitations. List a plan of events at the bottom that could help you write the invitation.

_____   _____

_____   _____

_____   _____

©Sheila Blackburn and Brilliant Publications

Connectives

Look at these words. They can connect two parts of a long sentence. Choose a good connective to go into each sentence for Stewie's diary for Mr Melling. If you can think of better connectives, you should use your own.

> when   where   and   suddenly
> unhappily   soon   eventually
> beacause   so

I was really pleased _____ Alfie gave me an invitation. It was

also a surprise _____ I don't usually get invited to parties.

_____, I had to calm down for lessons and it wasn't easy.

_____, I rushed home to see what Mum said and _____ I showed her

the invitation, she was happy for me to go. _____, the big day

arrived and off I went on a bus to the other side of town. _____ I

left Alfie's present on the bus which was a shame as Mum had gone to a lot of

trouble to get it. There was nothing I could do, _____ I went into the Zoomwell

Kart track and told Alfie's Mum. _____ she said it didn't matter and took

me to join the others. I had a fantastic time and _____ Dad picked me up

in his old van.

> excitedly   embarrassingly
> then   unfortunately   luckily

Stewie Scraps Top Secret – Teachers resource sheets for Stewie Scraps

Heads and tails

Making sentences make sense is fun! Especially when you read your sentence and realize that something isn't quite right!

The sentences below have been split in half and then muddled up – could Grandpa have had something to do with it? Can you help put them back together again?

Alfie Battersby invited Stewie _____

Stewie worried that _____ . _____

Flo was worried about _____

Sadly, Stewie left the gift _____

The karting went very well and _____

Back at home, Stewie set to work _____

He got very upset and angry when _____

Grandpa saved the day and _____

Stewie took the trolley cart to the park and _____

_____

Grandpa said that he used to race his carts with a family of _____

_____

… had a great time racing it with a girl	… showed Stewie an alternative design.
… boys and their sister, years ago.	… he found out he needed an engine.
… to his karting party.	… what to buy Alfie for a present.
… his Mum would not let him go.	… on the bus because he was so excited.
… designing his own go-kart.	… Stewie won a silver trophy.

©Sheila Blackburn and Brilliant Publications
Stewie Scraps Top Secret – Teachers resource sheets for Stewie Scraps

Who said that? – Speech marks

There is a lot of dialogue throughout this story and it all needs to be carefully punctuated. Look at all the examples of the things different people have said. Write each one next to the correct character picture, put in the speech marks and any other punctuation you feel is necessary.

Here take it its for you

Wow

Why are you out of breath

Looking good Bugzy

There knew id find you here

Here we are Stewie heres everyone

First some safety rules then a short
    lesson

Short for Constance Hate it like your
    trolley cart

Hello its stewie isnt it

Comprehension

1. Why do you think Alfie had to keep telling Stewie to take the invitation (pages 5–6)?

2. Read pages 11–12. What do you think Stewie is worried about?

   Can you say why he might feel this way?

3. Stewie is looking forward to the karting party (page 15), just as much as the other boys, but for very different reasons. Explain the different ways the boys are excited at the thought of the party.

4. Why do you think Stewie snaps the book shut (pages 20–21)?

   What does Grandpa mean when he says "it could have been worse"?

Comprehension (continued)

5. What has happened to Poppy's Saturday job and why (page 22)?

6. Look at page 23, say what has made Stewie look horrified?

7. Stewie thinks about Grandpa helping him with past projects (page 25) and thinks he might let Grandpa help with his cart idea. Say why Grandpa would like to be involved.

8. Why do you think Flo made sure Stewie was bathed and squeaky clean (page 27) before the party?

   What do you think about the birthday present she got for Alfie?

Comprehension (continued)

9. As he arrived at the karting place, Stewie was feeling very grown up – can you think why (page 28)?

What on page 29, made that feeling change very quickly?

10. Stewie talks very quietly and Mrs Battersby talks gently (pages 31–32). This tells us a lot about how Stewie was feeling. Write down some of the feelings that Stewie probably had when

... he went into the karting place.

... he met Alfie's Mum

... he saw the food tables.

11. Describe how the teams were chosen on page 37.

©Sheila Blackburn and Brilliant Publications

Comprehension (continued)

12.   Why did Stewie crash into the straw bundles at the side of the track (from page 39)?

13.   Explain why (page 45) the boys were patting Stewie on the back as he left the karting track.

14.   Why do you think that Bugzy scuttled off into the shadows of the shed (page 48)?

15.   Read page 49. What problems does Stewie have with his kart design?

16.   How does Grandpa, on page 52, save the day and become part of Stewie's project?

Comprehension (continued)

17.   Read through page 58. How does Connie know so much about racing the trolley cart?

18.   Why do you think Stewie goes shivery (page 62) when Grandpa talks about his old friends?

19.   Do you think Stewie will see Connie again? Explain your thinking.

20.   Even though Grandpa missed the afternoon's fun with the trolley cart, Stewie thinks he's a great Grandpa. Why do you think he feels this way?

©Sheila Blackburn and Brilliant Publications

Stewie Scraps and the Giant Joggers

Giant Joggers

Stewie goes on an overnight school trip. It is his first time away from home and his first time in the countryside. His head is full of ideas for making this and making that.

Back at home, there's a surprise birthday party for Grandpa and a welcome home for Stewie.

Grandpa's present is a new pair of slippers. "Could you get me a new pair of legs to go with them?" he jokes.

In the dead of night Stewie sits bolt upright. He knows exactly what his next design is going to be.

Find out what Stewie builds and why he ends up in a mess of grass, leaves and twigs in the shed!

Teacher's notes

Task sheet 1 Exclamation marks and question marks
- Discuss and identify known punctuation marks, and what they are used for.
- Introduce the ! and ?. If not known, look for examples in this text.
- Write some examples on sticky notes and group them together, so that pupils can identify any similarities (eg, opening words in questions or shorter sentences for exclamations etc).
- Model the task.
- Model how extra ideas can be generated from the text – this could include some oral drama work by hot-seating Stewie to elicit responses and ideas.

Task sheet 2 Words to use instead of 'said'
- Read chapter 1 together.
- Discuss what dialogue is.
- Ask the children to find sentences that have dialogue.
- Look how dialogue is written (ie: speaker first or last) and words that are used around it (said, or something different).
- Collect examples on sticky notes and group into ones that use said and others.
- Explain that the verb said helps to keep the text simple and easy to read – but that alternatives improve style and add interest.
- Think about the impact of using words instead of said.
- Make a collection of alternative words and then consider the impact that they have (ie: adding to atmosphere, mood of characters and indicators of ways to read and use intonation and expression).
- Model the task.
- After completion, read out the sentences, using said.
- Read the answers again with the alternative words, varying tone accordingly.
- Encourage expression and feeling and link to use of ? and ! previously.

Task sheet 3 Using commas in lists
- Read the first two chapters again, playing a game of signals for punctuation already encountered: eg click for a full stop, clap for an exclamation mark.
- Make a fist for question mark and finger on lips for a comma.
- Recap and reinforce what punctuation is used for.
- Ask if pupils know what the comma is for – if none know then explain.
- Make up a sentence that has a list of things and requires commas, cut up the words and ask pupils to arrange them in order – then draw commas on sticky notes and ask pupils to place them within the list to separate the items.
- Discuss what you have done so far.
- Explain and model the task. (You might want pupils to write out the sentences for themselves, rather than simply add the commas.)

Task sheet 4 Developing a character – Bugzy
- Read chapter 3 onwards/skim for parts where Bugzy is involved.
- With each sighting, make notes/key words that show what Bugzy is doing and what sort of friend this shows him to be. This should be a joint/group/paired task, depending on the children.
- Discuss what has been collected.
- Use dramatic conventions such as hot-seating to find out more of Stewie's actual feelings towards Bugzy – encourage/model focus questions.
- Model the task and provide support words for writing.
- Share the writing and ask the children to comment on each other's ideas and (if appropriate) to ask questions of each other.

Teacher's notes (continued)

Task Sheet 5 Framing and asking questions
- Read pages 58–63.
- Refer to work on ? previously and especially to words used at the start of the questions.
- Mind shower the sorts of things the giants might like to know about Stewie – stress that they obviously trust him, but can still be inquisitive.
- Model the task – and when they are finished, encourage the children to share and comment upon their work.

Task sheet 6 Writing in the first person
- Skim/ scan the text for references to Bugzy and discuss with the children – look for his actions and reactions so that pupils can consider what such a small creature might feel.
- Discuss what is understood by first/third person writing and give examples of each from other texts or by changing some of the current text verbally (eg: using the giants' view, similar to the previous task).
- Model how a third person sentence can be changed to first person and do more until the children are comfortable with the concept.
- Model the task, using points from skimming above.
- When completed, encourage the children to share their writing and comment constructively on each other's work, with particular reference to whether it was easy to write in the first person.

Comprehension
- 17 questions to assess and evaluate how well each pupil has understood the book.

Exclamation marks and question marks

When Stewie arrives at the countryside centre to stay overnight, there are lots of things he needs to ask and lots of other things that amaze him.

Sort the phrases below and add them to the correct rucksack. Add three more of your own ideas in each section.

Where will this fit

Fantastic

Will this work

Can I make it better

Look at that

Amazing

No time for football

This is great

What does this do

How does this work

©Sheila Blackburn and Brilliant Publications

Words to use instead of "said"

Choose the best word from the shapes at the bottom of the page to complete each sentence.

"You can go on the school trip overnight!" _____ Mum.

"Thanks, Mum! Thanks, Dad!" Stewie _____.

"There are so many ideas for things to design and make!" _____ Stewie.

Someone _____, "Are you coming to play rounders, Stewie?"

"Sorry! No time for sports," Stewie _____.

"We're going for a long walk this afternoon," Mr Melling _____.

"My legs ache!" someone _____.

"How long till we get back?" _____ another of the class.

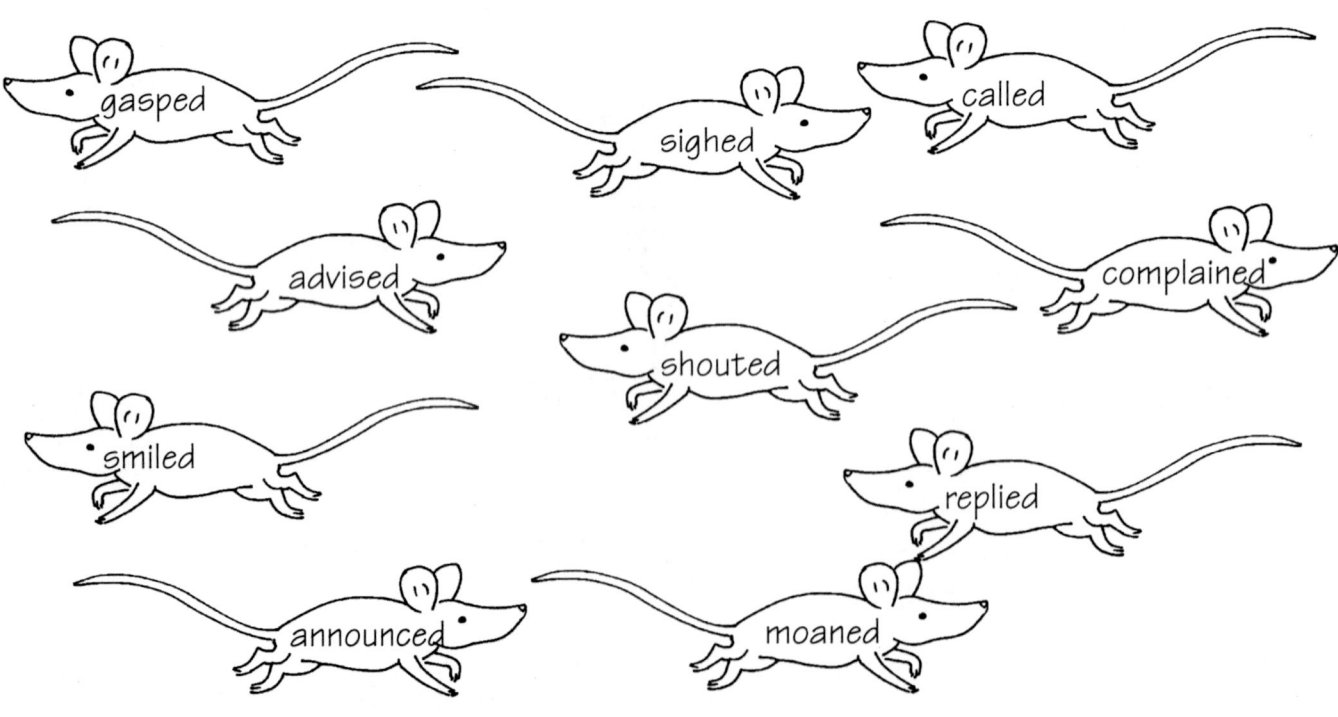

Using commas in lists

A comma gives us chance to take a short breath in long sentences. This is especially important where there are lists of things.

Look at each sentence and add commas where there are many things to separate. The rule is not to put a comma before the final and.

In JJ's van Stewie had travelled round the town to other towns and even to a big city.

Stewie felt surprised excited amazed and glad when he heard he could go on the school trip.

The coach trip was long hot and very noisy.

Stewie was trying to eat his lunch and look around take it all in and plan things in his head.

Stewie wanted to design a serving truck a trainer gadget a picnic table bin a tree den a bird hide and an obstacle course.

On the long walk the children moaned groaned grumbled and complained.

Stewie loved the fields the hedges the woods and the hills.

The children enjoyed sports drawing painting a treasure hunt and a quiz at the centre.

Before he went home Stewie planned a packing machine a shoe finder a sock sniffer and a toast delivery system.

The team games included balancing passing building paddling and climbing.

©Sheila Blackburn and Brilliant Publications

Developing a character – Bugzy

Stewie relies on his pet rat for company. Bugzy is always there for him. First, draw a picture of Bugzy in the frame on the sheet. Next, try to think of ways that Stewie would talk about Bugzy and describe him..

This is Bugzy, he's my best friend. Let me tell you about him, he's …

_____

_____

_____

_____

_____

_____

Framing and asking questions

The Giants explain to Stewie what they are doing – they seem to know all about him, but suppose they had a question to ask him, what might they ask?

Framing and asking questions (continued)

Now turn
this sheet over and
draw the giant
from the rivers and lakes.
What question would he
like to ask Stewie?

Stewie Scraps Top Secret – Teacher's resource sheets for Stewie Scraps

Writing in the first person

The story is told in the third person. Imagine that it's time for Bugzy to have his say and to write about his feelings and what happens to him.

Write Bugzy's account of what has happened.

Comprehension

1. On page 5, show what evidence there is to suggest that Stewie might not like the countryside.

2. Why did Stewie think he might not be able to go away on the school trip?

3. Look at all Stewie's design ideas on pages 8, 9 and 15. Which one is your favourite? Explain why.

4. Stewie is a hero to his class mates (pages 16 and 17). Why is this so special for him?

5. In the shop (page 20), why might Stewie try not to think of green fields and steep hills?

Comprehension (continued)

6.   Stewie isn't worried by Clint's note on the bedroom door. How do we know? Stewie was supposed to be banned from the bedroom. Stewie and Grandpa were banned from the kitchen, but behind each ban different things are happening. What are they?

7.   How does Grandpa react to his present?

8.   Who has given Stewie the idea for his next invention (page 30)?

9.   What do you think Stewie means by *a working breakfast* (page 33)?

10.   On page 44, Stewie is disappointed – what do you think should have happened?

Comprehension (continued)

11. What two things might Stewie have in mind when he says the joggers are for *Big* walks?

12. What seems to make the joggers work?

13. On page 61 the giant says "when all the rest look away". Who do you think he is talking about?

14. In the chapter *A bumpy landing*, why does Bugzy *go carefully, very carefully*?

15. What clues does Grandpa have that Stewie has been out on the joggers?

Comprehension (continued)

16.   What might Stewie mean when he says to Grandpa: "I can't say…" ?

17.   Grandpa asks Stewie to go for a normal walk on page 68. What does this tell you about what Grandpa thinks of Stewie's latest invention?

Stewie Scraps and the Star Rocket

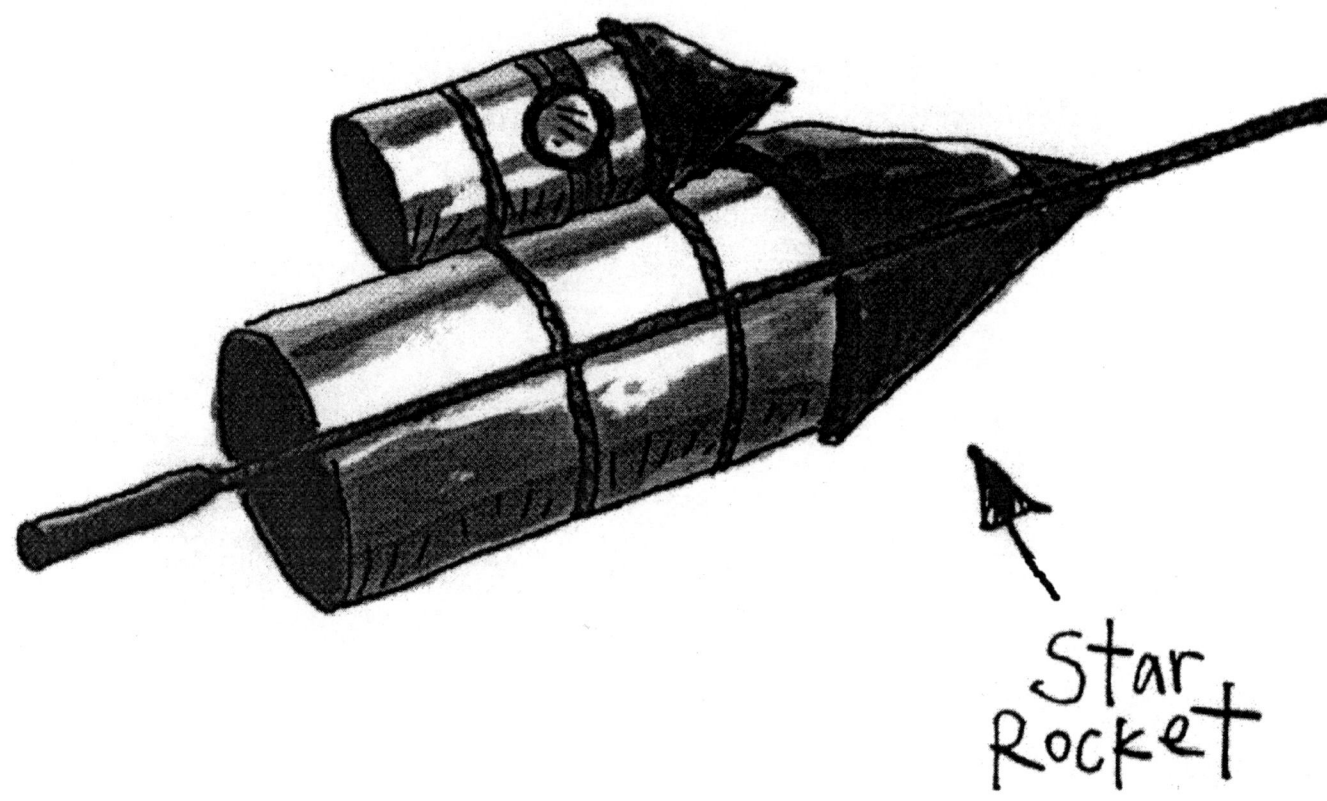

Star Rocket

"You still like fireworks, don't you, Stewie?"

On Friday 5th November, Grandpa's local pub is holding a fireworks party for charity. "You could come with me." Grandpa suggests.

Stewie thinks about it. Maybe it would help refine his Super Star Rocket design.

Stewie is spellbound by the firework display. He's never seen such big rockets before.

The next day, it takes only a couple of hours to find all the bits needed for his Super Star Rocket. But what will happen when Stewie tries to launch it?

Teacher's notes

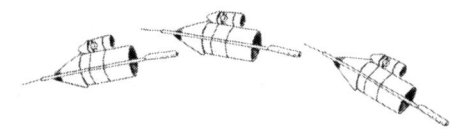

Task sheet 1 Considering and building upon a character – Grandpa

- Discuss what is meant by character.
- Talk about some famous book or TV/film characters and what makes them interesting.
- Read the instructions together.
- Read and discuss the box of words about Grandpa – can you identify pages in the story where these qualities are seen?
- Read through the sheet and the sentence openers – again use page references to identify relevant sections.
- Model the task and check if pupils need further support words to help them.
- After completion, check the children's responses/encourage peer marking and assessment.

Task sheet 2 Writing labels for diagrams

- Discuss non-fiction texts and the use of diagrams and look at examples together.
- Check that the arrows on such diagrams are accurately placed.
- Show how good labels will give more than just a name of a part matched to the labels – and therefore to explanations.
- Read the instructions together.
- Model one part of the task, showing how to refer to the text for support.
- After completion, discuss or compare labels to evaluate and possibly improve.

Task sheet 3 Making notes – Stewie's secret desgn book

- If available, look through note books and talk about notes as memory aids.
- Discuss how these differ from instructions on how to do something – it might be useful, for example, to model a set of instructions for firing a rocket, to be compared with the key words about the design of the rocket launcher.
- Read the instructions together.
- Having modelled the task above, make sure that pupils understand how to use page references to support their task.
- After completion, discuss or compare labels to evaluate and possibly improve

Task sheet 4 Keeping a diary as a record – Stewie's busy weekend!

- There are lots of reasons for keeping records and dairies – as a starting point, ask the children to think of some and share their ideas.
- Discuss why might this apply to Stewie.
- Read the instructions together and check that the children can follow the chart layout.
- Model how to access information from the text and identify the main events – these should be noted in the final column.
- After completion, encourage pupils to share their work and give reasons for their choice of ideas in the end column.

Teacher's notes (continued)

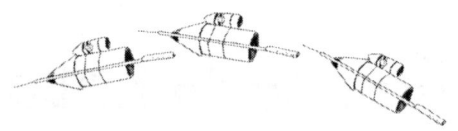

Task Sheet 5 Exciting verbs
- Discuss verbs, their function and how to identify them (put the word 'I' in front of them – one good way).
- What happens when verbs are taken away? Or when very ordinary verbs are used:
  Use the sentence: Stewie went along the street
  Identify the verb
  Use sticky notes to substitute more exciting verbs and think about improvements to the sentence and meaning.
- Read the instructions together.
- It might be useful to read the phrases or to limit the ones to be done – some pupils might need this differentiation if the long list is overwhelming.
- Model at least the first one and decide how spellings are to be given/checked.
- After completion, share some of the best ones, as identified by the children from their own writing.

Task sheet 6 Adventurous adjectives
- Discuss adjectives, their function and how to identify them.
- What happens when they are taken away? Or when very ordinary ones are used:
  Use the sentence: Stewie raced along the street
  Is there an adjective? Where would it go?
  Use sticky notes to add possible adjectives and think about improvement to the sentence and meaning.
- Read the instructions together.
- It might be useful to read the phrases or to limit the ones to be done – some pupils might need this differentiation if the long list is overwhelming.
- Model at least the first one and decide how spellings are to be given/checked.
- After completion, share some of the best ones, as identified by the children from their own writing.

Comprehension
- 21 questions to assess and evaluate how well each pupil has understood the book.

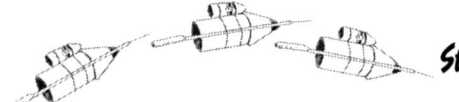 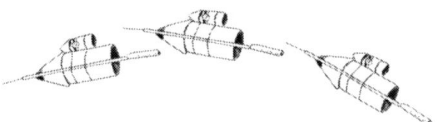

Considering and building upon a character – Grandpa

Carefully draw a picture of Grandpa in the cameo shape. Then reread pages 5–10, 21, 27, 61 –63 and complete the sentences at the bottom of the page. The words in the box might help you.

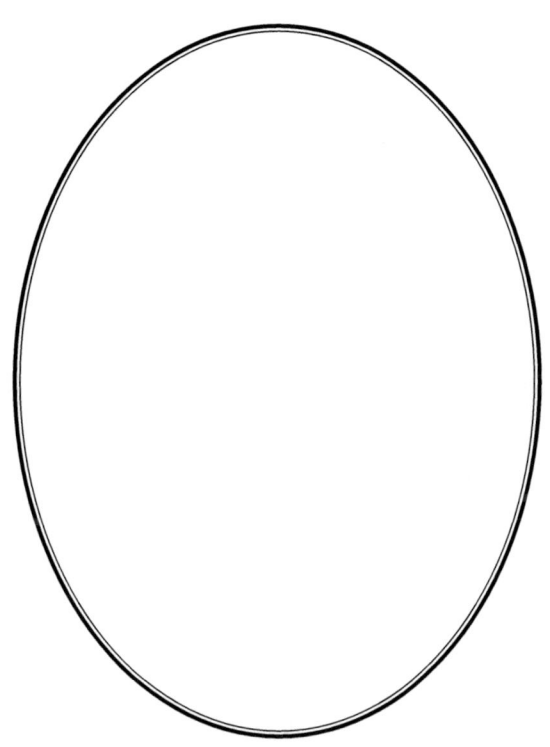

wise	understanding	reliable	friendly	calm
practical	a peacemaker	mischievous	quiet	funny
	set in his ways	easy to talk to		

In November, Stewie thought that Grandpa _____

On November 5th, Grandpa was happy because _____

After the firework display, Grandpa wanted _____

It's obvious that Grandpa has lots of time for Stewie because _____

Grandpa was holding the rocket tube. He seemed _____

Grandpa asks the same questions as Stewie. It makes me think that maybe Grandpa _____

©Sheila Blackburn and Brilliant Publications

 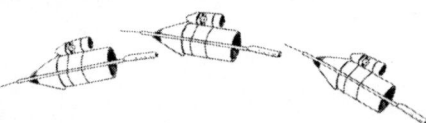

Writing labels for a diagram

Look closely at Stewie's diagram on page 17. Draw it as carefully as you can in the box below. Look at where the arrows point and make sure that you put the arrows in the same places on your diagram. Using the text to help you, write labels for each section of the Star Rocket.

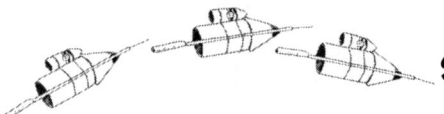 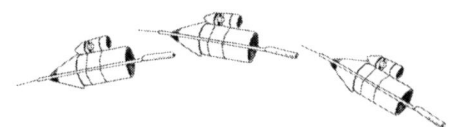

Making notes – Stewie's secret design book

We already know Stewie hates writing but sometimes he has to make notes to help him remember things. Look at the title in each box below. Find the page in the story and look at what it tells you about the item. Look at the illustrations too. Now draw your own illustration for each item. Add some notes or key words that will help Stewie to remember important information about each of the items.

Passenger pod	Oil-drum barbecue

Rocket launcher

Complete the flow chart that Stewie might draw for a rocket using the information given to you on page 24.

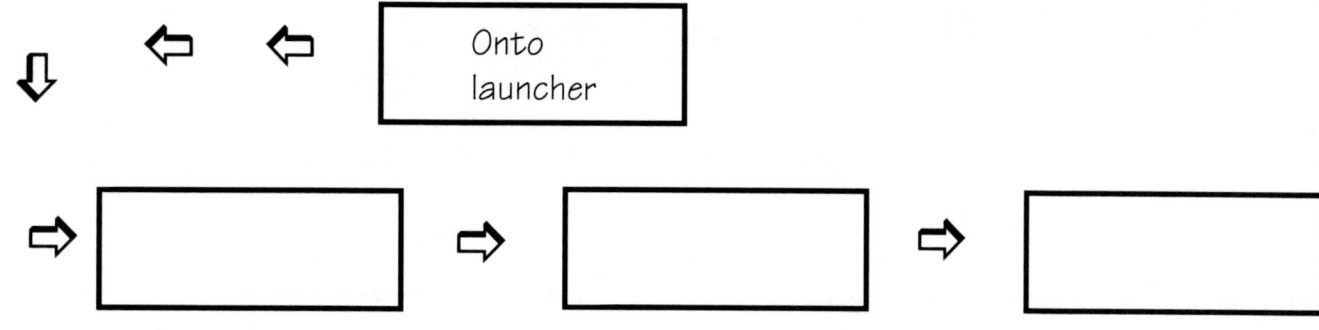

©Sheila Blackburn and Brilliant Publications

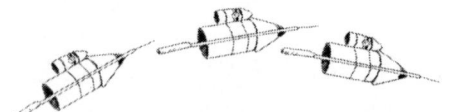 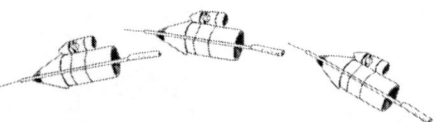

Keeping a diary as a record – Stewie's busy weekend!

Stewie has a very busy few days. Look at the chart below – it is a way to record things when they happen. Decide what information you need from the story and how you can find it. Fill in the chart, using words in the story to help you.

Page	Date	Time of day	What happened
	Friday 5th November	Afternoon	
	Friday 5th November	Evening	
35	Saturday 6th November	Morning	
	Saturday 6th November	Late morning	
37	Saturday 6th November	5 o'clock	
38	Saturday 6th November	5.25pm	
39	Saturday 6th November	Early night	
56–57	Saturday 6th November	Late night	
	Sunday 7th November	Morning	

Stewie Scraps Top Secret – Teacher's resource sheets for Stewie Scraps

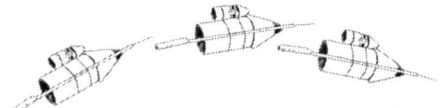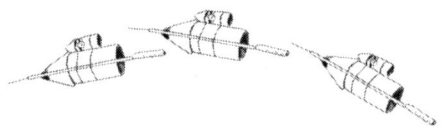

Exciting verbs

Look at the page references below. Find the given phrases by skimmimg and scanning the text. Highlight the verbs on the sheet. Add three more of your own that would be suitable or even better!

Pg 11	He pushed his way…	
24	The first rocket swished	
26	Fred was straining	
28	Grandpa tottered along the street	
35	The light filtered slowly	
34	He crept about	
39	Poppy sneered	
40	Stewie stole out the back door	
41	The moon hung about	
41	A single rocket stuttered	
44	The SSSR crackled and fizzed	
51	The down-suit puffed out	
52	The fire petals studded the black sky	
53	Stewie was swinging gently	

©Sheila Blackburn and Brilliant Publications

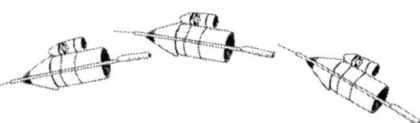

Adventurous adjectives

Look at each page reference. Find the given phrases by skimmimg and scanning the text. Highlight the adjectives on the sheet. Add three more of your own that would be suitable or even better!

5	Dull, dark and dreary days	
8	A flash firework display	
9	A few, little fireworks	
14	A new and amazing firework design	
15	Detailed labels	
19	A great experience	
23	Trails of spikey white lights	
24	A huge flower of red and gold	
27	Certain special details	
38	The rickety shed door	
41	A dull November moon	
42	The struggling Bugzy	
46	Tiny little bonfires	
46	Its mighty climb	
48	The critical time	
62	Battered and blackened old tube	
63	A very special firework	

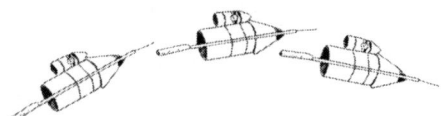

Comprehension

1. Read pages 5–7. Give three reasons why Stewie feels "down" at the start of the story.

2. Describe the sort of firework party Stewie thinks he'll have with his family, like in previous years (pages 8–9).

3. List (from page 10) all the reasons Grandpa had for inviting Stewie to the firework party at the pub.

4. "Trust grown-ups to let you down" (page 11). Why does Stewie feel let down by the grown-ups in his life?

5. Read pages 16 and 17. What sort of things motivate Stewie to write?

6. Stewie can be said to "have an answer for everything" and is very "matter of fact" about his answers. How does his reply to Mr Melling back up this view?

©Sheila Blackburn and Brilliant Publications

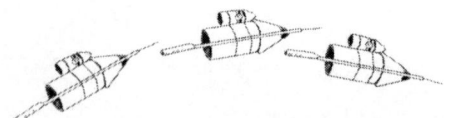 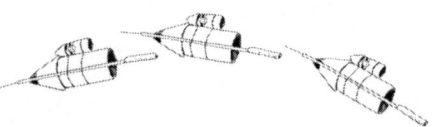

Comprehension continued

7. JJ's shop is useful to lots of people. How has it helped the pub where the firework party is being held?

8. Say what things fascinate Stewie at the party and why (pages 22 and 23).

9. Read through pages 22–25 and make a list of all the things that Stewie might put into his secret design book.

10. Stewie has to persuade Grandpa to go home (page 27). Give reasons why Stewie wants to go and Grandpa wants to stay.

11. Page 33 says "Bugzy felt uncomfortable, though he couldn't say why." This has a double meaning (it's ambiguous). Think of two things that are meant by the sentence.

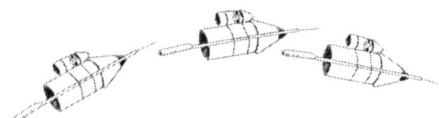 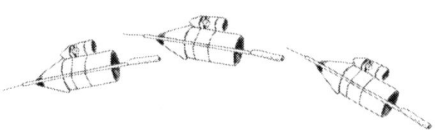

Comprehension continued

12. Why do you think Stewie needs secret access to JJ's glues and screws cupboard?

13. Explain the playful argument between Stewie and Poppy (page 39).

14. Which phrase tells you, on page 43, that Bugzy has worked out Stewie's plan for the rocket pod and the night sky?

15. Rockets from other gardens are described as fingers of coloured sparks. What could they be pointing at and why (page 46)?

16. Why do you think the red key button "looked like the top off a bottle of window cleaner" (page 49)?

©Sheila Blackburn and Brilliant Publications

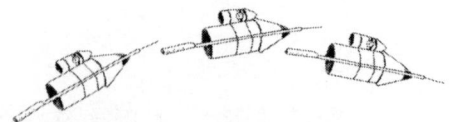
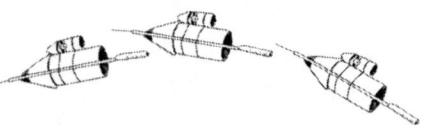

Comprehension continued

17. On page 55 the phrase "Dancing with the stars" is another one with a double meaning. Stewie is not about to dance with celebrities on TV, so what do you think he might mean here?

18. Give two reasons why the bouncy castle man was annoyed with Stewie.

19. Why is JJ annoyed the morning after Stewie's adventure?

20. There is a moment when Stewie thinks JJ is right. Why?

21. Finally, Grandpa changes Stewie's mind. How?

Stewie Scraps Top Secret – Teacher's resource sheets for Stewie Scraps

Lightning Source UK Ltd.
Milton Keynes UK
24 August 2010

158894UK00001B/2/P